DataOps

The Future of Data Lies in the Art of Automation

Fabrizio Zuccari

La scienza dei dati è il cuore pulsante del progresso, ma solo l'arte del DataOps può farlo battere in modo efficace.

The science of data is the beating heart of progress, but only the art of DataOps can make it beat effectively.

Sommario

Introduzione al DataOps

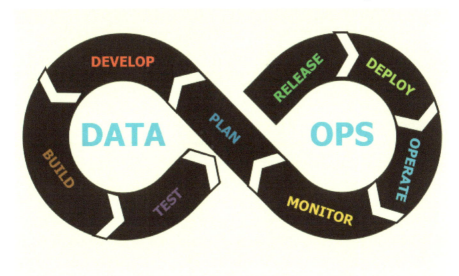

Agile, Lean Manufacturing, and DevOps are the components and main practices that define the DataOps approach for efficiently managing data-related work. Collaboration among software development, operations, and data management teams is the focal point for achieving the primary objectives of DataOps: improving data quality, increasing efficiency and management, while keeping an eye on further reducing errors.

DataOps: History and Definition

DataOps is a data management methodology that focuses on collaboration among different business functions to create efficient and scalable workflows for data management. In other words, DataOps combines the best practices of Agile, DevOps, and data management to create a flexible and scalable infrastructure for data management.

The Agile approach is focused on rapid response to

changes and continuous collaboration among stakeholders. On the other hand, DevOps emphasizes collaboration between software development and operations to deliver high-quality software with greater efficiency and speed. The combination of these approaches helps organizations improve their ability to manage and utilize data more effectively.

The history of DataOps can be traced back to 2014 when the concepts of DevOps and Agile were first applied to data management. However, the term "DataOps" was coined in 2015 by Jesse Anderson, a technology consultant specializing in big data. Anderson noticed that many organizations were struggling with data management due to inefficient processes and lack of collaboration among different business functions. To address these issues, he proposed the idea of adopting the Agile approach to data management.

In the following years, the concept of DataOps became increasingly popular among companies seeking to improve their data management. In 2017, a group of industry professionals founded the first DataOps community to promote the sharing of best practices and collaboration among stakeholders.

In 2019, the professional association Data Management Association International (DAMA) recognized DataOps as an emerging practice in the field of data management. Today, many organizations are adopting DataOps as part of their data management strategy. By adopting this approach, organizations can benefit from more efficient data management processes, faster release times, improved data quality, and enhanced customer experience.

DataOps: Objectives and Benefits

The implementation of DataOps provides a range of opportunities for businesses seeking to optimize their data utilization. Adopting a DataOps methodology means embracing an agile, collaborative, and data-centric approach to data management, governance, and analysis.

This approach allows for improved efficiency and quality in data management operations, as well as optimizing their utility in supporting value creation for the business. Here are some of the key opportunities offered by DataOps:

- *Improve Data Quality*
  Data quality is essential for the success of business operations. With the implementation of DataOps, organizations can enhance data quality through automation and standardization of data management processes. Additionally, DataOps enables quick identification of data quality issues and timely intervention for correction. For example, a marketing company can use DataOps to swiftly identify and resolve inconsistencies in customer contact data.

- *Speed up data analysis*
  DataOps allows the reduction of the time required for data processing, enabling organizations to make faster and data-driven decisions. By using automation tools for data processing, DataOps enables the quick and efficient analysis of large volumes of data. For example, an e-commerce company can utilize DataOps to rapidly analyse customer purchase data and identify buying trends.

- *Increase team's collaboration*
  DataOps promotes collaboration among teams, fostering increased efficiency and improved data quality. The DataOps approach encourages development, operations, security, and data analytics teams to work together to create an integrated data pipeline. This allows for more effective data management, knowledge sharing, and swift identification and resolution of issues. For example, a financial services company can use DataOps to integrate customer data from various sources and create a unified view of the customer.

- *Ensuring data security*
  DataOps helps ensure data security through the standardization of security processes and the implementation of automated security controls. Additionally, DataOps enables quick identification of data security breaches and timely action to resolve them. For example, a healthcare company can use DataOps to protect sensitive patient data and ensure compliance with data privacy regulations.

- *Support company innovations*
  DataOps promotes collaboration among IT, DevOps, Data Science, and business teams, fostering the sharing of knowledge and expertise. Through constant interaction among these teams, data management needs and issues can be identified more promptly. Furthermore, cross-functional collaboration enables the identification of the best solutions to address these issues and implement them more efficiently.

For example, let's consider a company that needs to improve data quality. Through the adoption of DataOps, the IT, DevOps, and Data Science teams can work together to identify the causes of data inaccuracies and inconsistencies. With ongoing collaboration, the teams can create a more robust and secure data pipeline to ensure data accuracy and reliability.

- *Increase operational efficiency*
  DataOps allows organizations to manage data more efficiently, reducing the time required to develop, test, and release new applications and features. Through automated pipelines and cross-functional collaboration, issues can be promptly identified and resolved, ensuring faster product release and improved time-to-market.
  For example, let's consider a company that needs to release a new sales management application. With DataOps, the IT, DevOps, and Data Science teams can collaborate to identify user needs and quickly develop a data pipeline that ensures accuracy of sales information. This way, the company can market the new application more swiftly while ensuring data quality.

- *Improve customer experience*
  Another significant opportunity offered by DataOps is the ability to enhance the customer experience. By collecting, analyzing, and managing data in real-time, businesses can have a comprehensive and detailed understanding of their customers' behavior. This allows them to tailor their products and services to meet customer needs and provide personalized and engaging experiences:

- *Personalization of the experience*
  One of the key advantages offered by DataOps in terms of customer experience is the ability to personalize the customer experience. Companies can use data to understand customer preferences and tailor their products and services to meet those preferences. For example, an e-commerce company could use customer purchase data to recommend similar or related products.

- *Customer retention*
  Effective data management enables businesses to identify customers who may be at risk of churning and take actions to retain them. For example, a telecommunications company could use call duration and usage data to identify customers who are utilizing the service less and offer them personalized offers to improve customer retention.

- *Improvement of customer satisfaction*
  DataOps can also enhance customer satisfaction. Data analysis can help businesses identify issues that customers may be experiencing with their products or services and take measures to resolve them. For example, a financial services company could use customer feedback data to identify areas where improvements are needed in customer service.

- *Optimization of user experience*
  Data can be used to optimize user experience on digital platforms. For example, a software

company could use data on the usage of its applications to identify pain points that users may be experiencing and make improvements to simplify the application usage.

- *Creation of a competitive advantage*
Lastly, DataOps can provide businesses with a competitive advantage in the market. By effectively collecting, analyzing, and managing data, companies can quickly adapt to customer needs and enhance the customer experience. This can help improve the company's reputation and drive long-term sales growth.

DataOps: Practices and Methodologies

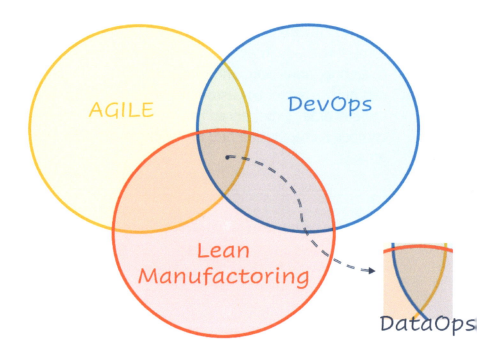

DataOps combines various practices and methodologies from the IT industry to create an end-to-end process for data management. Among the key methodologies used in DataOps are *Agile*, *DevOps* and *Lean Manufacturing*.

Agile:

Agile is a software development methodology based on collaboration, flexibility, and iterative delivery. The key concepts of the Agile methodology are customer centricity, collaboration, iterative delivery, adaptability, and continuous improvement. These principles aim to improve product quality, customer satisfaction, and software development process efficiency:

- **_Customer Centricity_**:
  Placing the customer at the centre of the software development process, involving them continuously throughout the development cycle.

- **_Collaboration_**:
  Promoting collaboration among all members of the development team, including stakeholders, testers, designers, and programmers, to ensure better project understanding and maximum development efficiency.

- **_Iterative Delivery_**:
  Facilitating iterative delivery, which involves breaking down the project into shorter development cycles, providing greater flexibility and the ability to modify and adapt the project based on the emerging needs of the customer.

- **_Adaptability_**:
  enabling adaptability to the needs of the client and the project, allowing for quick priority changes and timely project adaptations based on requirements.

- **_Continuous Improvement_**:
  enabling continuous improvement of the software development process through ongoing process evaluation and implementation of changes to enhance quality and efficiency.

DevOps:

DevOps is a methodology that aims to integrate development and operations aspects in the software lifecycle to deliver quality software quickly and reliably. DevOps was developed in 2008 and is based on the principles of collaboration, automation, and shared responsibility between development teams and operations teams, following the following principles:

- **Collaboration**:
  It promotes collaboration between developers and system operators, creating a culture of shared work and a team that works together to achieve a common goal.

- **Automation**:
  It is a fundamental aspect of DevOps as it helps reduce human errors and speed up the software deployment process. Automation can involve development, testing, release, and infrastructure management processes.

- **Continuous Integration (CI)**:
  It involves the continuous integration of developed code into a shared repository, allowing developers to quickly identify and resolve issues.

- **Continuous Delivery (CD)**:
  It involves the continuous and rapid release of software, enabling organizations to respond to customer needs more promptly.

- **Monitoring and Feedback**:
  It promotes continuous monitoring of software performance, allowing for the quick identification of any issues or malfunctions and providing immediate feedback to the developer.

Lean Manufacturing:

Lean Manufacturing is a production methodology that focuses on waste reduction and increasing the efficiency of the production process.

This approach was developed by Toyota in the 1950s and is based on reducing cycle times, minimizing waste, and eliminating non-value-added activities.
The concept of *waste elimination* is the central focus of the Lean philosophy, where waste is defined as *any activity that does not add value to the final product or service provided to the end customer.*
This means that the production process is optimized to reduce the time required to complete each step of the process and minimize the amount of waste produced. This, in turn, makes production more efficient and reduces costs.

The Lean methodology targets seven categories of waste: *overproduction, waiting, transportation, defects, over processing, inventory excess,* and *underutilization of skills.*

Lean Manufacturing also aims to eliminate non-essential activities and simplify the production process. This is achieved through the adoption of a continuous improvement approach involving all employees in the company and is based on data collection and analysis.

In the context of DataOps, the Lean methodology is used to create a lean and efficient data management process. Waste in data management, such as data duplication or collecting irrelevant information, is eliminated. The data management process is streamlined and optimized to reduce cycle times and improve overall efficiency.

MLOps

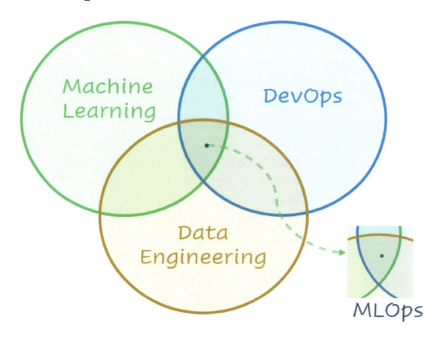

The concept of MLOps is an evolution of the DataOps concept: it applies DevOps practices and principles to the creation, management, and deployment of machine learning models in a scalable and reproducible manner. The complexity of building machine learning models requires continuous management of the model's lifecycle, from data acquisition to production, and MLOps encompasses the set of processes and technologies to ensure the quality, scalability, and security of the models. The first references to the concept of MLOps date back to 2015 when Google published an article on managing the lifecycle of machine learning models, introducing the concept of "Machine Learning Workflow." In 2017, Algorithmia published a white paper on the concept of "MLOps," describing how DevOps principles could be applied to machine learning model development. MLOps requires a range of tools and technologies to automate the workflow of developing machine learning models. These tools include model versioning systems, integrated development environments (IDEs), collaboration platforms, testing tools, deployment tools, and monitoring tools.

A concrete use case of MLOps could be the creation of a machine learning model for email classification as spam or non-spam. In this case, the MLOps process would involve establishing a continuous workflow that includes the following stages:

- **Data collection and pre-processing**:
  Collecting training and testing data from available sources, pre-processing the data for cleaning and normalization.

- **Model development**:
  Creating the machine learning model, selecting algorithms and machine learning techniques.

- **Model Validation**:
  Testing the model on a test dataset to evaluate its accuracy and performance.

- **Model Deployment**:
  Integrating the model into the production system and implementing a performance monitoring system for the model.

- **Continuous model management**:
  Updating and maintaining the model to ensure it continues to function properly over time.

The main tools used to support MLOps include:

- ***Model versioning systems:***
  Model versioning systems allow tracking the versions of machine learning models to facilitate collaborative development work and result reproducibility. The main model versioning systems include Git and GitHub. Git is a widely used distributed version control system in the software development world, while GitHub is a web-based platform that provides hosting functionalities for Git repositories.

- ***Integrated Development Environments (IDE):***
  Integrated development environments are software tools that provide a graphical interface for code development. The main IDEs used for machine learning model development include Jupyter Notebook and PyCharm. Jupyter Notebook is a web-based development environment based on Python that allows creating and sharing documents containing code, equations, graphs, and descriptive text. PyCharm is an IDE for Python application development equipped with advanced features for code debugging, testing, and refactoring.

- ***Collaboration Platforms:***
  Collaboration platforms enable collaborative work on machine learning projects, allowing code, data, and documentation sharing among team members. The main collaboration platforms used in the context of MLOps include Slack, Microsoft Teams, and Zoom. Slack is an instant messaging platform that allows creating thematic communication channels, sharing files, and integrating with other collaboration tools. Microsoft Teams is a collaboration platform that combines chat, video conferencing, and document sharing. Zoom is a video conferencing platform that

allows real-time collaboration with other team members.

- **Testing tools:**
  Testing tools enable evaluating the quality and performance of machine learning models. The main testing tools used in the context of MLOps include TensorFlow, Keras, and scikit-learn. TensorFlow and Keras are open-source libraries for developing machine learning models based on Python, while scikit-learn is a machine learning library for Python that provides tools for classification, regression, and clustering.

- **Deployment tools:** Deployment tools allow integrating machine learning models into the production system. The main deployment tools used in the context of MLOps include Docker, Kubernetes, and AWS Lambda. Docker is an open-source platform for creating, deploying, and running applications in containers. Kubernetes is an open-source container orchestration platform that enables managing the execution of distributed applications in a scalable and reliable manner. AWS Lambda is a serverless computing service offered by Amazon Web Services that allows executing code without managing the underlying computing resources. In the context of MLOps, AWS Lambda can be used to run machine learning models in a scalable manner without managing the underlying infrastructure. Additionally, AWS Lambda can be integrated with other AWS services, such as Amazon S3, Amazon DynamoDB, and Amazon API Gateway, to create complete serverless applications.

Other tools used in the context of MLOps include Apache *Airflow*, an open-source workflow orchestration system, and

MLflow, an open-source platform for managing the lifecycle of machine learning models.
Apache Airflow allows defining and scheduling complex workflows, while MLflow enables tracking machine learning models and managing their reproducibility and sharing among team members.

The choice of tools and technologies to use in the context of MLOps depends on the specific project requirements and the skills of team members. However, the combination of model versioning systems, integrated development environments, collaboration platforms, testing tools, deployment tools, and monitoring tools is crucial to automate the workflow of developing machine learning models and ensure result reproducibility, reliability, and scalability.

Embrace DataOps Culture

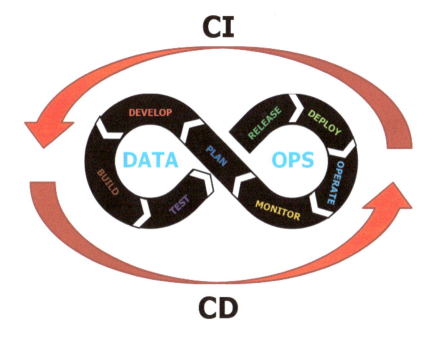

By focusing on a data ecosystem encompassing processes, technology, and teams, it is possible to promote an effective DataOps culture that maximizes the value of data and fosters harmony among diverse business teams.

Embracing the idea of DataOps as a continuous process that involves all parts of the company (and all personnel) becomes crucial for a successful future in business.

Based on the theory of DevOps, DataOps goes much further as it is more than just the merging of two related engineering disciplines.
It encompasses everyone, from the beginning of the data acquisition chain (from IoT devices to enterprise applications to third-party repositories) to all individuals

involved in shaping and transforming the data, and finally to those who use it in applications and analysis, as described in Hitachi Vantara's whitepaper, "*The Cultural Impact of DataOps: Collaboration, Automation, and the War on Silos.*"

Here are 5 key concepts related to adopting DataOps:

DataOps is a continuous process

This means understanding that data management is not a one-time project but an ongoing effort. It involves continuously collecting, processing, and analyzing data to identify patterns, trends, and valuable insights for informed business decisions.

By managing DataOps as a continuous process, companies can achieve greater agility and responsiveness to internal and market changes. This also requires a cultural shift towards data-driven decision-making by breaking down traditional silos and promoting collaboration among teams such as data scientists, developers, and business analysts.

The goal is to work together to define needs, build pipelines, and ensure that data is accurate, timely, and relevant. By doing so, the company can create a culture that values data as a strategic asset, leading to better business outcomes.

Supporting data-driven decision-making

To remain competitive in today's market, companies need to prioritize data utilization.
This means that all employees, regardless of their role, must recognize the value of data in their work.

By harnessing data, organizations can gain insights into customer behaviour, market trends, and internal operations, ultimately leading to better decision-making.

One example of prioritizing data utilization is in marketing. Marketing teams can use data to understand customer behaviour and preferences, allowing them to tailor their messaging and advertising efforts to specific audiences. Data analysis can guide the identification of the social media platforms where their target audience is most active, the type of content they engage with, and the time of day they are most likely to be online. By leveraging this data, the marketing team can create targeted campaigns that are more likely to resonate with their audience and increase engagement.

In addition to recognizing the value of data, companies should encourage open communication and sharing of data-supported insights. Employees should feel empowered to share their ideas and perspectives, but those ideas should be supported by data whenever possible. This approach helps ensure that the best ideas emerge, regardless of where they originate within the company.

For effective data-driven decision-making processes, leadership must relinquish some control. This means that employees at all levels should be empowered to use data to support their actions, and they should be provided with the necessary tools and training to do so. This way, companies can create a culture that embraces data-driven decision-making and promotes continuous evolution and growth.

Eliminating Data silos

To make this concept more tangible, let's consider a use case in a hospital setting. In a hospital environment, data is generated by various departments such as emergency, cardiology, radiology, and the laboratory. However, data from these departments is often isolated and inaccessible to other teams that may need it. For example, the emergency department may require access to a patient's medical history from the cardiology department to provide the best care. In the absence of accessible data, the emergency team may miss critical information that could impact patient care.

To break down these data silos, hospitals can implement a centralized data platform that integrates data from various departments. This way, all departments have access to a unified view of the patient's medical history, enabling better diagnosis and treatment. This approach requires collaboration between different departments and the establishment of governance policies that ensure the security and privacy of patient data.

The benefits of breaking down data silos can be applied to other industries as well. In the retail sector, a unified view of customer data can provide insights into customer behaviour, enabling targeted marketing campaigns and improving the customer experience. It is essential for companies to create a culture that values data sharing, with appropriate controls and access permissions in place, to enable data-driven decision-making.

Being bold and courageous

To successfully implement DataOps, companies must embrace a culture that is open to change and innovation. This means being willing to take risks and try new things. One way to do this is by adopting a more agile approach to data management. By breaking down silos and enabling collaborative work, companies can gain deeper knowledge of their data and make better decisions.

An example of a company that has successfully implemented DataOps is Netflix (more details can be found in the Use Cases chapter). Netflix is known for using data to drive business decisions, and its DataOps program is a critical part of its success. The company has built a culture that values data-driven decision-making and has heavily invested in the tools and processes necessary to make this possible.

Netflix's approach to DataOps is based on a set of principles that include breaking down silos, empowering teams, and embracing change. The company has created a centralized platform that allows teams to access and analyze data in real-time and has implemented a series of tools and processes to ensure data accuracy and freshness.

By adopting a bold and innovative approach to DataOps, Netflix has been able to stay ahead of its competitors and maintain its position as a leader in the entertainment industry. Other companies can take inspiration from Netflix by embracing a culture of innovation and investing in the tools and processes needed to effectively use their data.

Investing in the right tools

To ensure that data is utilized to its full potential, investing in the right data processing tools becomes crucial for companies to effectively share, access, and analyse data to support their business needs.

DataOps is not a single tool that can be purchased and forgotten: a DataOps solution should enhance collaboration, automate testing and monitoring, orchestrate data flows, and accelerate the deployment of new features. There are various tools available for building, orchestrating, and deploying data pipelines, depending on the resources and capabilities of the organization. In some cases, an all-in-one DataOps platform can provide advantages in terms of speed and agility (e.g., Talend, Databricks, StreamSets).

Proper training on the use of these tools is essential, and specialized external consultants can provide valuable advice to ensure a smooth transition to a successful DataOps culture. The focus should be on the data ecosystem, including teams, technology, and processes, to maximize the value of data and collaboration.

Embracing the continuous nature of DataOps processes is crucial to moving towards a successful future, and this mindset should be adopted by all employees.

Data management

Data management is a fundamental aspect of DataOps as it involves acquiring, preparing, storing, processing, and analyzing data effectively and efficiently:

Acquisition

The acquisition phase is a crucial aspect and involves identifying sources and collecting data from these sources. Here are some examples of use cases that illustrate how data acquisition can be implemented in a business context:

- **_Acquiring data from IoT sensors_**:
  A large manufacturing company is looking to improve its production operations using IoT sensors that monitor machines in real-time.
  These sensors generate a continuous stream of data, which is acquired and integrated into a data processing platform using communication protocols like MQTT or HTTP.
  The collected data is then used to analyze machine performance, identify any issues, and make informed operational decisions.

- **_Acquiring data from log files_**:
  An e-commerce company has a vast amount of log data generated by its web and mobile applications.
  These log files contain information about user interactions with the website or application, such as visited pages, used features, and response times.
  To acquire and integrate this data, the company can use data aggregation tools like _Apache Kafka_ or _Apache Flume_, which allow collecting log files from various sources and sending them to a data processing platform like _Hadoop_ or _Spark_.

- **_Acquiring data from databases_**:
  A telecommunications company uses multiple databases to manage customer data, such as account information, contracts, and customer interactions.
  To acquire this data, the company can use data

integration tools like Talend or Informatica, which enable connecting to different databases and integrating the data into a unified processing environment.
Once integrated, the data can be used to analyse customer activities, identify service issues, and improve the customer experience.

Data Preparation

Data preparation is another phase of DataOps where the collected data often requires a significant amount of work before it can be used for analysis.
In this phase, the data needs to be cleaned, transformed, and organized to be effectively utilized.
This includes cleaning to remove any errors and inconsistencies, removing duplicates, and reducing its size.

Examples of data preparation activities include:

- **Data cleaning**:
  Removing errors, duplicates, missing values, out-of-scale values, and outliers from the data.
  E.g.:
  if a company is collecting data on product sales, it may notice that some data rows have missing values. In the cleaning phase, the company should identify these missing values and decide whether to replace them with estimated values or remove those data rows altogether.

- **Data transformation**:
  Transforming the data into a standardized format that can be easily analysed and interpreted.
  E.g.:
  if a company collects data on sales from various sales locations worldwide, the data may be expressed in

different currencies. In this case, the company should transform the data into a single currency to simplify its analysis.

- **Data reduction:**
  Reducing the size of the data to facilitate management. **E.g.:**
  if a company is collecting large amounts of data that are not necessary for analysis, it may decide to eliminate some columns or aggregate them to reduce the overall size.

An example use case of data preparation is a company that collects customer information from various sources, such as websites, social media, and customer support services. The information may be collected in different formats and structures, making analysis challenging. In the data preparation phase, the company should clean and transform the data into a standardized format, removing any duplicates and reducing its size. This allows the data to be more effectively used for analysis and improving customer service.

Data Quality Control

Data quality control is a crucial aspect of DataOps as unverified or inconsistent data can lead to incorrect decisions and inaccurate analysis.
In this context, DataOps utilizes a range of techniques to ensure data quality. One of the techniques used for data quality control is consistency verification, which involves comparing data from different sources to identify any discrepancies or errors.
E.g.:
a company can use DataOps to verify the consistency of sales data between its accounting system and the payment data received from customers.

Another important aspect of data quality control is validation, which involves verifying data to ensure it meets quality requirements and conforms to business specifications.

E.g.:

a company may use DataOps to validate customer data to ensure it is complete and contains all the necessary information.

Data quality control can also include error identification and correction.
In this context, DataOps can utilize machine learning and artificial intelligence techniques to identify any quality issues and resolve them promptly.

E.g.:

a company may use DataOps to identify any anomalies in sales data and correct them before analysis

Data Storage

Data storage is fundamental in the DataOps process and involves secure and accessible storage of data.

E.g.:

a company may store customer data on its local servers. In this case, the storage phase would involve choosing suitable hardware and software to ensure security and availability to those who need it.

A common case involves the use of cloud storage services such as Amazon S3, Google Cloud Storage, or Azure Blob Storage. These services allow organizations to store large amounts of data on remote servers that can be accessed from anywhere with an internet connection. This approach has the advantage of reducing storage costs as organizations don't need to purchase and manage the necessary on-premise hardware.

Storing data on cloud storage services can offer greater flexibility for businesses as they can easily scale up or down the storage space based on their current needs (*dynamic scaling*).
E.g.:
company using a social media application may store images and videos uploaded by users on a cloud storage service. This way, the company can handle large amounts of data without worrying about the storage capacity of its own hardware.

In general, data storage is a critical phase of the DataOps process as data needs to be securely and reliably accessible.
Whether to use local servers or cloud storage services will depend on the specific needs of the organization, but both methods can be effective if managed correctly.

Data Processing

Another phase of the DataOps process is data processing, which aims to transform raw data into a more manageable and analysis-ready format. This phase can involve various activities, including aggregation, modelling, and information extraction.
E.g.:
a company using a website user activity monitoring system may collect a vast amount of raw data, such as users' IP addresses, the browser used, time spent on the site, and so on. However, this raw data is not immediately useful for analysis, so it needs to be processed to make it ready for use.

In this case, the data processing phase may involve

aggregating the data based on certain parameters, such as the number of site visits or the geographical origin of users. It may also involve creating models to identify patterns or trends in the data. For instance, the company may create a model to identify the times of day when website traffic is highest to better plan site maintenance.

Another common case involves extracting information from raw data.
E.g.:
a company using a production monitoring system may collect data on the machines used in production, such as activity and downtime times. The data processing phase may involve extracting information on which machines are the most efficient and which require more maintenance to improve production efficiency.

Data Visualization

The data visualization phase in the DataOps process focuses on interpreting the processed data and translating it into useful information for the organization. This phase can involve using various data analysis techniques, including statistical analysis, machine learning, and predictive analysis.

E.g.: *a company aiming to identify factors influencing customer satisfaction. In this case, the data processing phase may involve aggregating customer feedback data collected through surveys, emails, and social media. The analysis phase may then involve using statistical analysis techniques to identify the factors that most significantly affect customer satisfaction. This way, the company can identify areas for improvement and formulate strategies to enhance the customer experience.*

The use of data visualization tools is another important

aspect of the analysis phase.

A company may utilize data visualization software to create charts and diagrams that make it easier to interpret information and share it with other team members.

This way, the company can improve collaboration between departments and make more informed decisions.

Data Security

Data security is a critical issue that requires utmost attention in every phase of the data lifecycle. In DataOps, data security needs to be effectively and efficiently managed to ensure data protection against internal and external threats. By adopting best practices and appropriate security strategies, businesses can ensure data security and protect their customers and employees from data breaches and cyber threats.

Common Threats in DataOps

Among the common threats to data security in DataOps are:

- ***Internal threats:***
  These can arise from team members with unauthorized access to data or violations of security protocols;

- **External threats:**
  These can come from hackers or cybercriminals attempting to penetrate systems to steal valuable data;

- **Malware attacks:**
  These can cause irreversible damage to data or even disrupt the entire IT infrastructure of the organization;

- **Phishing attacks:**
  These can be used to trick users into revealing their login credentials, allowing hackers to access data.

Best Practices

To ensure data security in DataOps, there are some fundamental best practices to follow, including:

- **Access Controls:**
  Use role-based access controls to limit data access only to authorized personnel.

- **Encryption e Data Masking:**
  Use encryption to protect sensitive data and data masking to safeguard user privacy.

- **Data Backups and Disaster Recovery:**
  Have a data backup and recovery plan in case of data loss or service interruption.

- **Regular Security Audits and Assessments:**
  Conduct regular security audits and assessments to identify any vulnerabilities in the security infrastructure.

- **_Employee Education and Awareness Programs_**:
  Educate employees on security protocols and sensitive data management.

Strategies for Data Security

To ensure data security in DataOps, there are several strategies that can be adopted, including:

- **_Security Culture_**: Create a _security culture_ throughout the organization by raising employee awareness of the importance of data security and best practices.

- **_Security Policies_**: Establish comprehensive security policies that define security protocols and procedures to ensure data security.

- **_Specific Tools_**: Use advanced security tools such as cloud security systems, code security solutions, firewalls, and endpoint security solutions to protect data.

- **_Collaborate with specialized resources_**: Collaborate with security experts and professionals to develop a tailored security strategy for the organization and obtain technical support and security consulting.

- **_Continuous Security Monitoring_**: Continuously monitor IT infrastructure and applications to detect any suspicious or abnormal activities and take timely action to prevent damage.

- **_Identity and Access Management_**: Implement an identity and access management system to ensure that only authorized individuals can access sensitive data.

Scalability & Monitoring

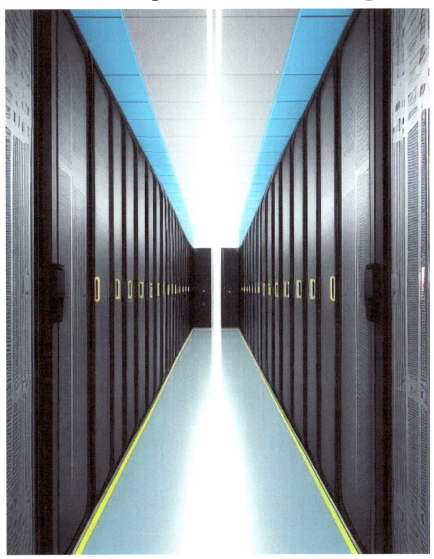

Scalability is a critical aspect of DataOps, which refers to the set of practices and tools used to manage and optimize the data pipeline from acquisition to delivery. As data volumes continue to increase at an exponential rate, organizations need to ensure that their data pipelines can scale to meet growing demands.

Scalability in DataOps means that the system can handle a growing amount of data and processing without impacting performance, reliability, or availability. In other words, it allows organizations to adapt to changes in data volumes, velocity, and variety, ensuring that the data pipeline can still deliver results in a timely and accurate manner.

Let's take an example to illustrate why scalability is essential in DataOps. Consider an e-commerce website that receives millions of transactions per day.
The website's data pipeline needs to acquire and process massive amounts of data, including customer orders, inventory data, shipping information, and more.
With increasing data volume, the data pipeline must be able to handle the additional load without degrading performance or causing downtime.

Without a scalable data pipeline, the e-commerce website may encounter various difficulties, including:

- *Slow processing times*: With increasing data volumes, processing times can become longer, which can impact customer satisfaction and lead to lost sales.

- *Downtime and system failures*: If the data pipeline cannot handle the increased load, it may become overloaded and cause downtime, resulting in revenue loss and loss of customer trust.

- *Limited growth*: If the data pipeline is not scalable, the organization may be limited in its ability to grow and expand its operations.

To address these challenges, organizations must design and implement a scalable data pipeline that can handle the growing volume of data. This may involve implementing distributed architectures, containerization, and cloud-based infrastructure that can scale up or down based on demand.

To achieve scalability in DataOps, a combination of best practices is required to address various aspects of the data pipeline, from design and architecture to deployment and management.

Next we will explore three critical best practices to achieve scalability in DataOps:

Distributed Architecture and Microservices

Distributed architecture and microservices are two essential components of a scalable data pipeline. Distributed architecture refers to the practice of breaking down a monolithic application or service into smaller, manageable components that can be deployed and scaled independently. Microservices are a type of distributed architecture that takes this concept to the extreme by breaking down a service into even smaller, self-contained modules that can be deployed and scaled individually.

By implementing distributed architectures and microservices, organizations can achieve the following benefits:

- **Improved scalability**: Since each component can be deployed and scaled independently, organizations can better manage their resources and handle variable demand levels.

- **Enhanced resilience**: If one component fails, it does not impact the entire system, reducing the risk of downtime and improving availability.

- **Increased agility**: With smaller and modular components, organizations can respond more quickly to changes in demand or requirements.

E.g.:
An e-commerce company may have a distributed architecture that includes microservices for product recommendation management, order processing, and inventory management. By breaking down these services into smaller and manageable components, the company can scale each service independently, allowing for more effective management of variable demand levels.

Containerization and Orchestration

Containerization and orchestration are two fundamental practices for achieving scalability in DataOps.

Containerization involves packaging an application and its dependencies into a self-contained and isolated unit called a container. Containers provide a lightweight and portable way to deploy applications and services, simplifying their movement between environments or scaling them up or down as needed.

Orchestration refers to the process of automating the deployment, management, and scalability of containerized applications. With orchestration tools like Kubernetes or Docker Swarm, organizations can automate the deployment of containers across multiple nodes, monitor their performance, and scale them up or down as required.

By implementing containerization and orchestration, organizations can benefit from the following advantages:

- **_Improved scalability_**:
  Containers can be easily scaled up or down, facilitating the management of variable demand levels.

- **_Increased agility_**:
  With containers, organizations can quickly deploy and move applications between environments, enabling them to respond rapidly to changes in demand or requirements.

- **_Enhanced resource utilization_**:
  Containers allow organizations to maximize the utilization of their resources by running multiple applications on the same host without compromising performance.

_E.g._:
A large financial services company might utilize containerization and orchestration to deploy and manage its trading platform. By containerizing the application and its dependencies, the company can easily move it between environments and scale it up or down as needed, ensuring they can handle variable demand levels during peak trading hours.

Cloud-Native Infrastructures

Cloud-Native Infrastructure refers to the practice of designing and building applications and services optimized for cloud environments. This involves utilizing cloud-native technologies such as serverless computing, managed services, and elastic scaling to build and deploy applications.

By implementing cloud-native infrastructure, organizations can benefit from the following advantages:

- **_Improved scalability_**. Cloud-native technologies are designed to handle variable demand levels, simplifying the scaling of applications up or down based on needs.

- **_Increased agility_**. With cloud-native infrastructure, organizations can quickly deploy and move applications between cloud environments, enabling them to respond rapidly to changes in demand or requirements.

- **_Enhanced resource utilization_**: Cloud-native infrastructure allows organizations to maximize resource utilization by running multiple applications on the same cloud instance without compromising performance.

_E.g._: _A media company might use cloud-native infrastructure to deploy and manage its streaming platform. By leveraging serverless computing and managed services, the company can quickly deploy and scale its application, ensuring an optimal streaming experience for users._

The importance of monitoring in DataOps cannot be underestimated. Without proper monitoring, organizations cannot effectively manage their data pipelines, detect any issues before they become critical, or optimize performance.
Next we will explore the significance of monitoring in DataOps and discuss some key best practices for effective

monitoring.

To monitor a data pipeline effectively, organizations need to track a set of key metrics that provide insights into performance, utilization, and availability. Some of the most important metrics to monitor include:

- **Data ingestion rate**: The rate at which data is being ingested into the pipeline.

- **Data processing rate**: The rate at which data is being processed within the pipeline.

- **Latency**: The time taken by data to traverse the pipeline.

- **Error rates**: The number of errors or failures occurring within the pipeline.

- **Resource utilization**: The amount of CPU, memory, and storage being utilized by the pipeline.

By tracking these metrics, organizations can gain insights into the performance of their data pipeline, identify bottlenecks and areas for improvement, and act to optimize performance.

Monitoring tools

To effectively monitor a data pipeline, organizations need to have the right tools and processes in place. Some of the most important tools for effective monitoring in DataOps include:

- **Logging e Alerting**:
  Logging and alerting tools are crucial for quickly

identifying and responding to issues. By setting alerts for key metrics and logging errors and exceptions, organizations can ensure they are notified of problems as soon as they occur.

- **Performance monitoring:**
  Performance monitoring tools allow organizations to monitor key metrics in real-time, enabling them to identify and address issues before they become critical. These tools can also provide insights into usage patterns and help organizations optimize their data pipelines.

- **Infrastructure monitoring:**
  Infrastructure monitoring tools enable organizations to monitor the performance of their underlying infrastructure, including servers, databases, and networks. By monitoring key metrics such as CPU usage, memory utilization, and network latency, organizations can identify and resolve issues that may impact the performance of their data pipeline.

By implementing these tools and processes, organizations can effectively monitor their data pipelines, quickly identify and resolve issues, and optimize performance over time.
E.g.:
An healthcare company may use logging and alerting tools to monitor the performance of its patient data pipeline. By monitoring key metrics such as data ingestion rate and latency, the organization can identify issues and take action to optimize performance, ensuring that patient data is available when needed. Additionally, the organization can use infrastructure monitoring tools to monitor the performance of its underlying infrastructure, identifying and resolving issues that may impact the pipeline's

performance.

Cloud-based Infrastructures

The use of cloud-based infrastructure for DataOps has become increasingly popular in recent years as more organizations recognize the benefits of transferring their data operations to the cloud.

Let's explore the advantages of cloud-based infrastructure for DataOps and discuss some of the best practices for utilizing cloud-based infrastructure.

Cloud Computing

Cloud computing provides on-demand access to a shared pool of computing resources, including servers, storage, and applications. By using cloud computing for DataOps, organizations can easily scale their infrastructure up or down, paying only for the resources used. Cloud computing also provides built-in redundancy and disaster recovery capabilities, ensuring that data pipelines remain available and reliable.

Infrastructure as Code

Infrastructure as Code (IaC) is the practice of using code to manage and automate infrastructure provisioning. By using IaC tools like Terraform or CloudFormation, organizations can easily create, modify, and delete cloud-based infrastructure resources in a consistent and repeatable manner. This can help ensure that the infrastructure is deployed correctly, reducing the risk of configuration errors and minimizing downtime.

Serverless Architecture

Serverless architecture is a cloud computing model that allows organizations to build and manage applications without the need to manage servers. By using serverless computing for DataOps, organizations can focus on creating and managing their data pipelines, rather than worrying about infrastructure management. This can help reduce costs and improve agility, as organizations can quickly deploy new features or functionality without worrying about the infrastructure.

Managed Services

Managed services are cloud-based services that are managed and maintained by the cloud provider. By using managed services for DataOps, organizations can offload the burden of managing infrastructure, databases, and other services to the cloud provider, allowing them to focus on their core business functions. Managed services can also provide integrated security, compliance, and monitoring features, helping organizations ensure that their data pipelines are secure and reliable.

Elastic Scalability

Elastic scalability is the ability to automatically scale infrastructure resources up or down based on demand. By using elastic scalability for DataOps, organizations can ensure that their infrastructure can handle sudden spikes in usage, minimizing costs during periods of low demand. Elastic scalability can also help ensure that data pipelines remain agile and scalable, allowing organizations to easily expand their cloud infrastructure as they grow and expand. This can be particularly beneficial for organizations anticipating rapid increases in data volume or workloads in the future.

However, using cloud infrastructure for DataOps requires some key best practices to ensure success: companies should implement proper security controls to protect sensitive data during transmission and processing. Additionally, a backup and recovery strategy should be adopted to ensure that data remains available in the event of system failure or natural disasters.

Companies that properly implement cloud infrastructure for DataOps can gain numerous benefits, including increased agility, scalability, security, and cost reduction. However, it is important to be fully aware of the risks and challenges associated with using cloud infrastructure and adopt appropriate best practices to mitigate them.

Performance Test

Conducting performance testing is an essential step to ensure the scalability and monitoring of DataOps operations. Performance testing activities are crucial to ensure that the infrastructure and software can handle expected workloads and adapt to unforeseen situations. Various performance testing techniques, such as load testing, stress testing, benchmarking, and performance profiling, provide valuable insights into system performance and can help organizations identify and address any issues before they can cause service disruptions or security problems.

- *Load Testing*
  Load testing is a type of performance test that simulates user traffic and measures system performance under different loads. Conducting load testing allows organizations to identify the maximum number of users or transactions the system can handle without performance degradation. This information can be used to optimize the infrastructure and software to ensure it can handle expected workloads.
  E.g.:
  A social media company can conduct load testing to ensure their data pipeline can handle a spike in user

activity during a major event like the Super Bowl.

- **Stress Testing**
  Stress testing is a type of performance test that simulates extreme workloads to identify the breaking point of the system. Conducting stress testing allows organizations to understand how the system behaves when pushed beyond its limits. This information can be used to optimize the infrastructure and software to handle unexpected workloads.
  E.g.:
  A financial services company can conduct stress testing to ensure their data pipeline can handle a sudden influx of transactions during a market crisis. With stress testing, they can identify any bottlenecks in their data pipeline and ensure it can handle the increased workload.

- **Benchmarking**
  Benchmarking is a type of performance test that measures system performance against industry standard benchmarks or competitors. Conducting benchmarking allows organizations to identify areas where they can improve system performance and identify potential optimization areas.
  E.g.:
  A healthcare company can conduct benchmarking to compare the performance of their data pipeline against industry standard benchmarks. They can use this information to identify areas where they can

improve the performance of their data pipeline and optimize their infrastructure and software.

- **Performance Profiling**
  Performance profiling is a type of performance test that identifies areas of the code or infrastructure that are causing performance degradation. Conducting performance profiling allows organizations to identify any bottlenecks and optimize performance.
  E.g.:
  An e-commerce company can conduct performance profiling to identify any areas in their data pipeline that are causing performance degradation. They can use this information to optimize their code or infrastructure to ensure their data pipeline is performing at its best.

- **Capacity Planning**
  Capacity planning is the process of determining the resources needed to handle expected workloads. This process helps organizations ensure they have the necessary infrastructure and software to handle expected workloads and scale resources up and down as needed. Capacity planning can help ensure that the infrastructure is properly sized to handle workloads of different sizes and also prevent underutilization of resources, which can be an additional cost for the organization.
  E.g.:
  An e-commerce company may conduct capacity planning to ensure they have enough resources to handle sales during peak seasons like Black Friday.

They can use the collected information to determine the resources needed to scale the infrastructure and ensure service availability.

Continuous Improvement

Adopting a mindset of continuous improvement is essential to ensure the success of DataOps operations. By embracing agile methodology, DevOps practices, continuous integration and delivery, feedback loops, and data-driven decision making, organizations can continually improve their processes and ensure that their data flow operates at its best.

- **Agile Methodology**
  Adopting an agile methodology is crucial to fostering a mindset of continuous improvement in DataOps. By adopting an agile methodology, organizations can quickly adapt to changing requirements and identify areas where they can enhance their processes.
  E.g.:
  A healthcare company can adopt an agile methodology to ensure they can respond rapidly to patient needs. They can use this methodology to continuously improve their data flow and ensure they provide the best possible care to their patients.

- **DevOps Practices**
  Adopting DevOps practices is vital to fostering a mindset of continuous improvement in DataOps. By embracing DevOps practices, organizations can bridge the gap between development and operations and ensure the delivery of high-quality software and

infrastructure.

E.g.:

A financial services company can adopt DevOps practices to ensure they can quickly respond to continuously evolving market conditions. They can use this methodology to continuously improve their data flow and provide their customers with the best possible service.

- **Continuous Integration and Delivery**
  Embracing continuous integration and delivery is crucial to fostering a mindset of continuous improvement in DataOps. By adopting continuous integration and delivery, organizations can quickly deliver new features and infrastructure enhancements, ensuring they maintain high-quality standards.

  E.g.:

  An e-commerce company can adopt continuous integration and delivery to ensure they can quickly respond to continuously evolving market conditions. They can use this methodology to continuously improve their data flow and provide their customers with the best possible shopping experience.

- **Feedback Loops**
  Embracing feedback loops is essential to fostering a mindset of continuous improvement in DataOps. By incorporating feedback loops, organizations can gather input from users and stakeholders and use that feedback to continuously improve their processes and infrastructure.

E.g.:

A social media company can embrace feedback loops to ensure they provide their users with the best possible experience. They can use this methodology to continuously improve their data flow and ensure they deliver relevant and engaging content to their users.

- **Data-Driven Decision Making**
  Adopting data-driven decision making is crucial to fostering a mindset of continuous improvement in DataOps. By utilizing monitoring and data analysis tools, organizations can collect and analyze information about their processes and infrastructure. This enables them to identify any issues or inefficiencies and take appropriate measures to address them.
  E.g.:

  A telecommunications company may use monitoring tools to gather information about network performance. If these tools indicate an increase in dropped calls or latency, the company can take steps to improve the quality of service provided.

Some Use Cases

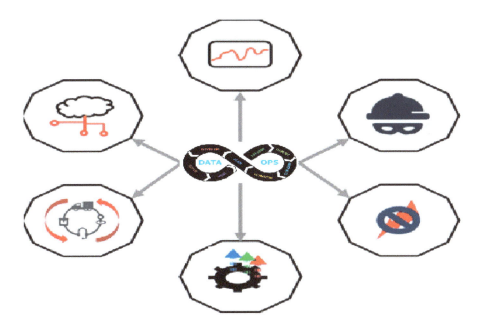

Netflix

The entertainment platform has developed the concept of DataOps to improve efficiency and speed in implementing machine learning algorithms, creating a platform called **Metaflow** that simplifies the entire machine learning development pipeline, including data management, model development, model management, and model deployment in production. The Metaflow platform has been developed with a DataOps mindset, where the focus is on creating a lean and agile development and deployment environment.

Here are some details about what has been developed:

- ***Simplification of the development workflow***: Metaflow simplifies the process of developing machine learning algorithms by providing a centralized platform for managing all stages of the development lifecycle. The development platform allows developer teams to easily manage data collection, model development, validation, testing, and release activities.

- ***Automation of the development process***: The platform utilizes automation for creating development workflows, managing computing resources, and automatically updating machine learning models in production.

- ***Data and model quality control***: The development platform incorporates data monitoring tools, data quality control tools, and model validation tools to ensure accuracy and quali.

- ***Scalability of the development pipeline***: Metaflow enables scalability of the machine learning development pipeline by utilizing scalable computing resources and dynamically managing computing resources based on processing needs.

For more information about Netflix's DataOps solution, Metaflow, you can visit the following link: https://metaflow.org/.

LinkedIn

The popular social media platform has implemented a DataOps solution called **Data Hub**, which simplifies enterprise-level data management and ensures real-time access and quality. This means that the data quality is continuously monitored and improved as it moves through the development pipeline.
Here are some details about Data Hub:

- **Simplification of data management**:
  The data management platform allows teams to easily manage access, sharing, and searching of data in a centralized location.

- **Automation of the development process**:
  The platform utilizes automation for creating data development workflows, managing computing resources, and automatically updating data in real-time.

- **Data quality control:**
  The data management platform incorporates monitoring tools, quality control tools, and validation tools to ensure accuracy and quality of the data.

- **Data access and sharing**:
  The platform enables teams to easily share data with

other teams and access the data they need to perform their work.

For more information about LinkedIn's DataOps solution, you can visit the following link: https://engineering.linkedin.com/blog/2019/data-hub

The Washington Post

The renowned news organization has implemented the DataOps solution "**_PostHaste_**" to improve data quality and collaboration among teams. They have created a collaboration platform based on Slack that allows teams to share data and information in real time. The platform also integrates quality control tools and data review capabilities to ensure accuracy before publication.

PostHaste manages a wide range of data-driven applications, including:

- News analysis applications,
- Election data collection and analysis,
- Tools for advertising and user engagement.

The solution has improved development speed and reduced the time required to implement new data-driven features.

Here are some details on how PostHaste has been implemented:

- The project was developed internally by the engineering team at The Washington Post and released as open source for the community.

- The solution is based on Kubernetes, a container orchestration tool that simplifies the deployment and management of applications in cloud environments.

- It offers an intuitive graphical user interface that enables data and development teams to easily create complex data pipelines and run them in a Kubernetes environment.

- t also integrates various open-source technologies to streamline data management, including:

  - Apache *Airflow* for workflow management,

  - Apache *Superset* for data visualization

  - Apache *Arrow* for data processing.

- It provides data versioning capabilities, allowing teams to easily monitor and manage changes.

Metlife

The American insurance company has adopted DataOps to streamline the data development process and ensure the agility of the data development infrastructure.

With the implementation of DataOps, Metlife has created a centralized data development platform that includes real-time monitoring, management, and quality control tools.

The data development platform also incorporates automation tools, such as ETL process automation, to simplify the data development workflow.
This platform is capable of developing and deploying data-driven applications more quickly while ensuring quality and accuracy

Here are some details about MetLife's DataOps solution:

- Implementation of a Hadoop-based data analytics platform: This enables the processing of large amounts of data and the generation of detailed analytics in a more efficient manner.
  The platform utilizes a range of open-source tools, including:

  - Apache *Spark*,

  - Apache *Kafka*,

  - Apache *NiFi*

- Establishment of a DataOps Center of Excellence: MetLife has created a DataOps Center of Excellence to promote the adoption of best practices and automated processes for data management. The center has developed a set of tools and frameworks to simplify the data development and deployment process within the company.

- Implementation of an automated data pipeline: MetLife has implemented an automated data pipeline that helps streamline much of the data development and deployment process. This pipeline leverages tools like Jenkins to automate the creation and distribution process, reducing the time required for manual execution.

- Utilization of monitoring and analysis tools: MetLife employs monitoring and analysis tools to track the performance of its platform and identify any issues. These tools include, among others:

  - *Grafana*

  - *Kibana*

- Use of an IT task automation platform: MetLife utilizes an IT task automation platform that incorporates tools such as Ansible to automate the installation and configuration process for data processing services.

Cedars-Sinai

Cedars-Sinai, a major hospital and medical research center, has implemented DataOps to manage the data workflow and improve collaboration between teams. They have created a data development platform that utilizes real-time monitoring tools and quality controls to ensure data accuracy and readiness for use.

The solution also supports a development infrastructure

that enables teams to work collaboratively, sharing data and information in real time through communication tools like Slack. This approach has enhanced collaboration between teams, reduced development time, and improved the quality of data used in healthcare and medical research.

The solution was developed in collaboration with a consulting firm, Databricks, and is based on the Databricks Unified Data Analytics platform. The DataOps team used Databricks tools to automate the entire data workflow, from collection to preparation, analysis, and publishing.

The main goal of this initiative was to improve access to clinical data and efficiency in data management. Previously, they relied on various data silos and manual processes to access and manage clinical data. With the DataOps solution, the team was able to consolidate all the data into a single platform, eliminating the need for manual steps and increasing the speed of accessing information.

The result has been faster information processing times and increased efficiency in managing clinical data. Furthermore, the platform has strengthened the security and compliance of clinical data, ensuring that it is only accessed by authorized personnel.

Etsy

Etsy is an e-commerce company that has adopted DataOps to manage the vast amount of data generated by its operations. They have created a real-time data management system that collects and analyzes information from customer interactions with the website and mobile app.

Etsy's solution is based on the use of Apache Kafka, a distributed streaming platform that enables real-time data processing and analysis

This architecture utilizes a set of open-source tools for data processing and analysis, such as:

- *Apache Beam*
- *Apache Flink*
- *Apache Druid*

Etsy has also developed a custom graphical user interface (GUI) that allows employees to access data and execute queries more efficiently.

This GUI allows access to a wide range of data, including:

- Product information
- Customer data
- Marketing data
- Sales information

The adoption of DataOps has enabled Etsy to achieve faster and more accurate data analysis, as well as reduce latency times between data collection and processing/analysis. This has improved the customer experience and allowed for more informed and timely business decisions.

Etsy described its DataOps solution in a 2018 article titled "*Data on the fly: Building an Event-driven Data System*".

Capital One

Capital One, a major American bank, has implemented a DataOps solution to enhance data management and operational efficiency. Capital One's DataOps solution is called the "Enterprise DataOps Platform," which has been built to integrate the capabilities of a variety of open-source tools
Among them:
- *Apache Spark*
- *Apache Airflow*
- *Apache NiFi*
- *Hadoop*

The platform has been implemented to enable centralized data management and efficient distribution to business teams, providing real-time visibility into the status of information and related activities.
The solution features a collaborative and self-sufficient management model that empowers business teams to make quick, data-driven decisions.

Implementing DataOps

Before starting to implement DataOps in your company, it is important to consider a series of prerequisites such as:

- Defining the company's objectives.
- Forming a dedicated team.
- Adopting suitable technologies and tools.
- Managing development and delivery processes.
- Managing change.
- Continuously monitoring and analyzing.

- Providing continuous training and development for the staff.

The company should carefully plan the transition process. Implementing DataOps requires a structured and methodological approach that involves adopting a set of practices and processes.

Objectives and Requirements

Defining the objectives and requirements of the project is a crucial step in implementing DataOps in your company. Before starting any activity, you need to identify the business objectives and specific goals of the DataOps project. This step is essential because it will help you maintain focus on the big picture and work in a structured manner to achieve the goals.

To identify the objectives and requirements, you need to understand the company's business needs and define the specific goals of the project. For example, if the business objective is to increase sales, you could define a specific goal for the DataOps project, such as improving sales data analysis to identify market trends and sales opportunities.

Once the objectives are defined, you need to identify the data requirements necessary to achieve them. These data requirements may include the data source, data quality, data update frequency, and other factors that are important for data analysis.

Additionally, you need to recognize the challenges that may hinder the achievement of the business objectives. For example, there may be a lack of skilled personnel in data management or issues with data quality. Identifying these challenges will help you consider them during the design and implementation process of the DataOps project.

Finally, it is important to define the success metrics of the project. These metrics will help you evaluate the success of the project and identify any areas that require improvement. Success metrics may include reducing data development and deployment time, increasing the efficiency of the data management team, or improving the accuracy of data analysis.

DataOps Team

The first thing to do is to identify the necessary roles and skills required to form a successful team. This involves identifying roles such as DataOps engineer, data analyst, data scientist, project manager, and delivery manager.

Once the roles are identified, it is important to find the ideal candidates for these positions. The members of the DataOps team should have extensive experience in data management, software development, and operations, along with a strong understanding of the company's business objectives and customer needs. Additionally, they should be able to work collaboratively and transparently, have a solid understanding of Agile methodologies, and possess a customer-oriented mindset.

A successful DataOps team should also have the ability to work autonomously and make informed decisions in a timely manner. This requires defining clear roles and responsibilities and creating a work environment that encourages collaboration and knowledge sharing.

Furthermore, the DataOps team should be able to work with various stakeholders, including the company's IT and business teams. Collaboration between these teams is crucial to ensure that the data management solutions developed by the DataOps team meet the needs of the company and its customers.

Tools & technologies

The technologies and tools used in the implementation of DataOps are another important element to consider. These tools should be designed to support collaboration and automation of data development and management activities.
The technologies should also be capable of supporting data integration and the creation of data pipelines.

Some of the common DataOps tools include Apache **Kafka**, Apache **Hadoop**, Apache **Spark**, and Apache **Airflow**. Data quality tools such as **Talend**, **Informatica**, and **DataRobot** are essential for ensuring data accuracy and consistency. Other tools that can be used include **Tableau** for data visualization and monitoring, and **Jira** for project management and team collaboration.

The choice of the right tools depends on the specific needs of the company and its clients, as well as the availability and skills of the DataOps team.
Once the tools are selected, it is important to integrate them into a continuous workflow that enables end-to-end data management, from data collection to final delivery.

It is crucial that the tools are carefully selected based on their ability to support transparency and collaboration among teams. Open and transparent communication is essential for the success of DataOps implementation, so the tools should support information sharing and collaboration among team members, including developers and data scientists.

Processes of Development and delivery

The development and delivery processes that respect the principles of Agile methodology must be defined and adopted in order to ensure maximum efficiency, speed of delivery, and data quality.

The development processes should be organized in a way that maximizes collaboration among DataOps team members, as well as between different teams, such as data scientists and software developers. Collaboration between teams should be supported by collaboration tools such as *Slack*, *Asana*, or *JIRA*.

As for the delivery processes, the main goal is to quickly deliver data to those who need it while maintaining the integrity and quality of the data. For this reason, it is important to implement an automated data pipeline system that ensures fast and reliable delivery.

The development and delivery processes should involve careful planning of activities, with the involvement of all stakeholders, in order to ensure maximum efficiency and reduce the risk of errors.

The development and delivery processes in DataOps should be designed to:

- Maximize collaboration between teams
- Respect the principles of Agile
- Ensure fast delivery and data quality
- Plan activities carefully
- Implement an automated data pipeline system.

Change Management

Change management is a crucial aspect of implementing DataOps. It is important to involve internal staff, effectively communicate the benefits of the change, manage risks, and constantly monitor the results to ensure that the change is achieving the set objectives.

Without proper management, the adoption of new practices and technologies can be challenging and may not yield the desired results.

Here are some important steps to follow to ensure effective change management:

- **Understand the context and challenges:** Before initiating any change process, it is important to understand the context and challenges being faced. This can include understanding current data management practices, technologies being used, challenges hindering the achievement of goals, and desired outcomes. This understanding will help guide the change strategy.

- **Involve internal staff:** Involving internal staff is crucial for effective change management. This can be done through training, education, and participation in the development and implementation processes. This way, employees will have an active role in creating new practices and technologies.

- **Effective Communication:** Communication is an important aspect to ensure effective change management. It is important to communicate the value of DataOps and how it can improve current data management practices. This can be done through meetings, presentations, webinars, and other forms of communication.

- **Risk Management:**
  There are always risks associated with change, so it is important to manage them properly. This can include identifying potential risks and creating contingency plans to address them.

- **Evaluation & Monitoring:**
  It is important to assess the outcomes of the change and monitor progress to ensure that desired results are being achieved. This can be done by creating success metrics and analyzing data to evaluate the effectiveness of the new practices and technologies.

Monitoring & Analysis

Monitoring and analysis should be implemented from the beginning of the project. To ensure accurate monitoring of performance and outcomes, companies need to use the right tools: performance monitoring tools can be used to monitor system performance in real-time and identify any issues or anomalies. Additionally, analysis tools can be used to gather and analyze data to identify trends and areas for improvement.

The collected data can also be used to analyze DataOps processes and identify any inefficiencies or errors: performance monitoring data can be used to identify activities that require more time and resources and pinpoint DataOps processes that can be optimized.

Another use of analyzing the collected data is to help identify the causes of system issues and errors: analysis can assist in identifying the reasons behind increased response times or malfunctions.

Monitoring and analyzing data provide valuable insights into customer performance and data utilization by end-users: this information can help companies understand how data is being used and how it can be optimized to meet customer needs..

Training and Skill up

To effectively implement a DataOps-focused solution, it is crucial to have highly skilled and motivated personnel who can quickly and proactively understand new technologies and implemented processes.

Training and development of staff are essential elements of the DataOps implementation process: companies need to identify the skills and knowledge required for data management and cross-team collaboration. Subsequently, adequate training should be planned and provided to both existing resources and new hires.

Training can be delivered through formal training courses, webinars, workshops, or through assigning tasks that allow employees to learn in a practical manner.

Companies should promote a culture of continuous improvement where employees can acquire new skills and knowledge. This can be achieved through offering ongoing training programs, participating in industry conferences and seminars, or creating cross-functional workgroups.

By doing so, companies can foster innovation and enhance organizational agility.

References

Below are a series of publications and URLs to further explore the topic:

- Humble, J., & Farley, D. (2011). Continuous delivery: Reliable software releases through build, test, and deployment automation. Addison-Wesley Professional.

- Poppendieck, M., & Poppendieck, T. (2003). Lean software development: An agile toolkit. Addison-Wesley

- Kim, G., Behr, K., & Spafford, G. (2016). The Phoenix Project: A Novel About IT, DevOps, and Helping Your Business Win. IT Revolution Press.

- Kim, G., Humble, J., Debois, P., & Willis, J. (2016). The DevOps Handbook: How to Create World-Class Agility, Reliability, and Security in Technology Organizations. IT Revolution Press.

- Chen, W. T., & Lu, Y. (2018). From DevOps to DataOps: A new approach for data-driven decision making in a data-intensive organization. Journal of Database Management (JDM), 29(3), 1-21.

- Hassani, H., Ibbotson, J., & Alzahrani, B. (2020). The impact of DevOps and agile methodologies on data management. Journal of Cloud Computing

- "MetLife case study: How a US insurance giant transformed its data management with DataOps", TechHQ, 2020.

- "Cedars-Sinai Deploys DataOps Platform to Improve Data Quality, Access", Health IT Analytics, 2019.
- "How Michelin Is Leveraging DataOps to Boost Factory Efficiency", DZone, 2021.

- Chen H., Chiang R. H., & Storey V. C. (2012). Business intelligence and analytics: From big data to big impact. MIS quarterly, 36(4), 1165-1188.

- Kimball, R., Ross, M., Thornthwaite, W., Mundy, J., Becker, B., & Evans, J. (2013). The Kimball Group Reader: Relentlessly Practical Tools for Data Warehousing and Business Intelligence. John Wiley & Sons.

- Christopher Bergh, Gil Benghiat, Eran Strod (2020)The Data Ops Cookbook: Methodologies and Tools That Reduce Analytics Cycle Time While Improving Quality Datakitchen

- Zikopoulos, P., Eaton, C., deRoos, D., Deutsch, T., Lapis, G., & Brown, K. (2012). Understanding big data: Analytics for enterprise class hadoop and streaming data. McGraw-Hill Osborne Media.

- DataOps Manifesto: https://dataopsmanifesto.org/en/

- Guidelines on regulatory compliance and risk management (National Institute of Standards and Technology): https://www.nist.gov/topics/risk-management

- GDPR: https://eur-lex.europa.eu/legal-content/IT/TXT/?uri=CELEX%3A32016R0679

- CCPA: https://oag.ca.gov/privacy/ccpa